A HOUSE OF DAR VACATION

JENNIFER MILLER

Acknowledgments

I want to dedicate this book to my husband, **Rick.** There are no words to describe my love for you, but the one thing I really want to say is, thank you, for WANTING me, and for being my HERO!

Also, I want to say thanks to my parents, my amazing kids, my beautiful grandkids, my crazy aunt, and all my friends for all your constant support. I want to thank my family for all the hours you have had to listen to the insane ideas inside my head. Even though most of you think I need to be evaluated.

Cover Art by © Creative cover Designs
(Vicki Adrian) Artist

Beta Readers:

Lorene Palmer, Rick Miller, Ethel Nance.

Editors:

Partners in Crime Book Services, Randy Henry.

Photographs:

Brittany Henry & Rick Miller, Shutterstock.

Imaginational inspiration crew:

Jewel Shipley, Amanda Hall, Joann Herley, Vicki Adrian.

Chapter One
KIRA

"GIRLS, why does it seem like every time you're having fun, time flies? I can't believe we have already been here three days. It feels like it's been three seconds. Lord knows I can remember counting down the days back home, always in a rush to get to Friday and the weekend. Little did I know at the time, I was merely wishing my life away."

Luna plops down in the chair next to me. "I always dreaded harvest season. That time of year, the blazing sun seemed to cook us from the inside out. I swear, it would feel like I had been in the fields for days only to look at my watch only to find out it had been minutes. Because we were always in the sun back home whenever we got downtime, we would go camping in a cool, shaded spot. However, this is kinda nice in its own way. As far as I know, this is my first trip to the beach, and surprisingly, I am enjoying it."

"I had no idea I even needed this when XuL brought it up, but I will say the view is spectacular." Brit giggles.

I pull my sunglasses down so I can see the boys better. "They are easy on the eyes, that's for sure. I have to make myself look past all the muscles to even enjoy the scenery."

"Kira, how did you find this place?"

SAGE floats around us before settling in the chair next to Brit with a big hat on her head. "Kira didn't. I found this all on my own. Master DaR has been yelling for rotations about a vacation and I knew any old place wouldn't do."

"As usual, SAGE, you have outdone yourself. This place is an outdoor paradise, especially with all these huts sitting out in the water, like the luxury ones back home. Everyone is close enough to be together if they want, but far enough to be on their own to run around naked if they want to."

"I had a few Building bots come out several rotations ago to install and update several things such as this area we are all in, but for the most part, the rest remains untouched."

"I will say, I really do like it here."

"Kira, Master DaR has already requested that I look into acquiring the entire area so we can secure the property properly. If the purchase goes through, I will get all of you together so that we can customize each hut to your specific taste."

Hearing Keida scream, we instinctively turn back towards the water, watching XuL, throw her up into the air before landing back in the water with a huge splash. Raven is pacing alongside them, barking, and snarling as she is voicing her disapproval of their play fighting. The other hounds, Ghost, and Glory, seem content playing fetch on the beach with Katherine. Poor Thorn watches them all from a distance, still refusing to engage in much of anything after losing Ellaria.

Brit takes the bag of chips out of my hand and mumbles in between bites, "As big a fit as Raven is causing, you would think she would simply jump in the water to stop them."

"She knows they're playing, but it's apparent she still doesn't like it." We all watch as Danny walks closer to Raven, and when he reaches his wet hand out to pet her, she backs away pawing at the water. When he splashes her playfully, I swear if looks could kill, that Hellhound would have melted him on the spot. Especially with him laughing at her reaction. She stomps her feet on the ground and just as I think she is going to pounce on him, Raven turns, shaking all over as she heads back under one of the large shade trees, laying down next to Thorn, butting him lovingly with her head before settling down.

Brit points a chip at Thorn. "That poor hound is proof that animals get just as attached to us as we do to them."

"I overheard Katherine talking to DaR earlier. She is worried because he is starting to refuse to eat as well. All of us are at a loss as to what to do to help him. One minute he is playing with the others, then the next, it's like he just loses the desire to do anything. I personally think he needs a new person. You know, like how most go buy a new puppy, in hopes that it will help ease the burden of losing another."

"Did that ever work for you?"

"Nope."

"Me either."

Even in such a peaceful place, I become lost in my thoughts as the past suddenly lies heavily on my mind. I didn't realize I was staring out at nothing until Alana sits down on the end of my chair and lays her hand on my leg.

"Kira, quit. I can see the weight of the world scrolling through your mind, simply from the frown upon your face. Places like this are as wonderful as they are deadly. Instead of appreciating all this, the quiet and peacefulness allows your mind time to recap and replay the horrors you have experienced. That is not how it should work at all."

"Sorry, girls I didn't mean to be a Debbie Downer. Have either of you seen Ivy or Victoria this morning?"

Alana throws a long towel out and lays down in the sand at my feet. "Victoria and Tyberius are sitting in the shade under the veranda over there. I passed them on the way here. Vic said sunbathing was not her thing because her skin was too sensitive, so she was going to read some. And Ivy and AvX were sneaking off. I only know this because SoL was raiding the kitchen early this morning. I swear that man is always hungry. Anyway, he saw AvX in the main substance area with SAGE. They were packing food for a surprise picnic he had planned for Ivy. They were going hiking to one of the water-falls today."

"Mistress Alana, I have provided multiple chairs for our comfort. There is no reason for you to lay on the ground."

"SAGE my dearest, I'm totally comfortable, you need not worry about me. When you are at the beach, one must lay in the sand in order to get the full effect."

"I personally don't care much for the sand; it's hot, and it gets in everything. When you lay down on it, it magically attaches itself to places I don't particularly want it in. I had SCOUT remove it from our home world and replace it with soft grass that goes right up to the waterline."

Alana looks back up at us with a mischievous smile on her face. "SAGE, how do you know the sand gets everywhere? Have you and SCOUT been doing the dirty? Did he dive down on you for a taste test?"

I have to put my hand over my mouth to stop my laughter when SAGE says, "Excuse me?" She has no idea what Alana is referring to.

"SAGE, has your sexy, rough and brooding man been visiting the Venus fly trap between those silky legs of yours?"

"Mistress Alana, shame on you! We don't speak of such things, and anyway, I am not the type to kiss and tell."

All of us crack up, lord these girls are good for the soul.

"Sorry, girls, I got a little sidetracked there with dirty images of SAGE and SCOUT in my mind and almost forgot, Miya and Hugo are going to shuttle over later today as well."

SAGE stands up. "I knew I should have prepared that last cabin before coming out here. I will return shortly."

SAGE disappears just as I hear RaZ let out a big yell. He has snatched what looked like a big disk out of the air that DaR and SoL have been tossing back and forth while XuL was playing with Danny and Keida. We all laugh when RaZ skims a wing along the water's edge, completely soaking DaR in the process. With a big smile on his face, DaR shakes his head, flinging water everywhere before running a hand down his face.

Luna fanning herself suddenly has all of us laughing. "My goodness that man is too pretty for his own good."

"Yeah, I've noticed he isn't too shabby. Speaking of cuties, where is your Tordan? I thought he would be out there with the rest of them."

"If my eyes are not messing with me, I think he is sneaking up behind DaR as we speak. Last night we were talking about some of the things I enjoyed back home and I told him I always wanted to go snorkeling, but never got the chance. I know better than to mention anything I would like to do. Because now, he is determined to find the perfect place to take me. So, he has been out there swimming around all morning. I am not a fan of the water, or swimming, but I am willing to suck it up if he finds something he wants me to see."

Now that I am watching closer, I can see RaZ and Tordan working together to distract DaR. They both should know better by now that they can seldom get anything over him unless he wants them to. RaZ dives from above just as Tordan pushes up through the water behind him. In a split second, DaR has grabbed Tordan by the arm and slings his massive body right out of the water like he weighs nothing straight towards RaZ. Tordan and RaZ end up becoming a mass of legs and wings as they crash into the water tangled up together.

I can't help but smile when DaR starts laughing as he watches them struggle to untangle themselves. RaZ's huge ass wings flare out, pushing a wave behind him that ends up knocking Keida down. When she pops back up, coughing the water that went up her nose, Danny is instantly at her side making sure she is ok. If I was RaZ I wouldn't go over there right now.

By this time, it's a full-blown war in the water. XuL and RaZ gang up on SoL but he throws them around like they're rag dolls. Tordan and DaR who have been watching the other boys play are unexpectedly grabbed from behind by two red arms and thrown into the air. They both come up sputtering as Hugo laughs hysterically behind them. When all of them turn towards him, he starts rushing to get out of the water, but Tordan gets to him first. Wrestling like a bunch of kids, we all laugh when SoL grabs all three of them at once in a big bear hug before falling backward in a splash.

If it wasn't for all the laughter, you would be convinced a true battle was going on out there. When another wave knocks Keida over, she turns, ready to get into the skirmish herself, but before she can get to the others, Danny grabs her, doing his best to drag her out of the water as she fights against him.

Raven is back up on her feet, and the other hounds stop when she growls. Katherine has been standing on the beach watching them with her hands on her hips. We all gasp when RaZ suddenly launches out of the water, grabbing her before she can run away. He flies them high above the water, twirling her about, Katherine's laughter echoes all around us. I glance away for just a second when I see Miya walking towards us on the beach. "Come on up, we have plenty of room, and the view is quite entertaining."

Looking back, I sit up. RaZ is pretending like he is going to drop Katherine, and she is screaming playfully. However, I don't think either of them realize how high up he really is. Keida is still pulling against Danny's hold, and just as he turns, arguing with her, RaZ loses his grip on Katherine. Her screech has all of us holding our breath even as he dives after her.

I don't know who is more shocked at what happens next, as it all seems to happen in slow motion. Katherine is now only a few feet from the water, and because of the height she was dropped, there is no way this is not going to hurt when she hits. RaZ has turned instantly, diving for her, but we can tell he isn't going to reach her in time. Everything is happening so quickly that I almost miss it when Danny lifts his hand. In the blink of an eye, Katherine is surrounded in a bright blue glow that stops her inches from the water effortlessly.

RaZ unfortunately fails to stop in time and ends up crashing into the water hard. However, he is swiftly back on his feet, although his wing appears to be injured slightly. Katherine looks over at Danny and instead of him allowing her to fall into the water and get wet. He simply flicks his wrist and the glow that is surrounding her brings her safely back over to the beach. The moment her feet touch the sand. The blue glow disappears, returning to Danny. Everyone has stopped and is just looking at Danny as his eyes glow brightly. Katherine, being who she is, quickly diffuses the situation. "Take that RaZ, pick on me again and I'll sic Danny's ass on you."

"Now don't be like that sweet thing, I would have caught you."

"Is that before or after you crashed into me? That ending was quite graceful by the way. Go play with your brothers, they like to roughhouse. Thank you, Danny, for coming to my rescue."

"Anytime."

That's all the boy says as he walks away from everyone, Keida in tow, his entire body is still slightly glowing. Raven pushes her head against his stomach and that's when I realize he is no longer a kid because she used to tower over him.

"Brit, how old is Danny now?"

"I think he will be sixteen in a couple of months. Victoria wants to have a big party for him, but everyone knows how uncomfortable that would make him. So, I have been trying to think of something else to do instead. Danny is a quiet soul, that's for sure, and has never liked being the center of attention."

"I swear he has grown a foot since I last saw him, and is filling out quite nicely. He is going to be quite the looker when he matures."

"Yeah, that boy has become like a son to me. Recently, Keida and Danny have been arguing constantly. I sent him to Vic and TY's several times last week for the evening, just to have a moment's peace in the house. I think they spend too much time together and you remember what it was like at that age when your hormones were all over the place."

"XuL is still unhappy with the sleeping arrangements, I am assuming?"

"Oh, yeah, and he is getting more and more vocal about it the older they both get."

"Have you had that dreaded birds, and bees conversation with Keida yet? You know Danny is not the only one growing up here. Especially where she is not fully human, what is normal for us won't be for her. XuL's people mature much quicker than we do."

"No, … Kira, I have not. I am trying my best to put it off as long as I can. I can't help but wish she would remain innocent for as long as possible. We all know that's not going to happen, and pretending otherwise won't prepare her for the upcoming challenges she'll face, even if I am in denial about her growing up. I can remember my mother stumbling through that talk and at no point did she warn me about cute green alien guys."

We all laugh at that comment.

"All jokes aside, we couldn't pick a better guy for her than Danny, but just because they have always been hooked at the hip doesn't mean they are supposed to be more than that. I know this sounds terrible, but Keida only knows him. She should have the chance to shop a little if you know my meaning."

"Yes, I completely understand. Even though I don't see that in her future. Not only is he always an arm's length away, but she has twenty-three uncles. There isn't a guy in existence that could handle that. You have to admit Danny doesn't let the others intimidate him at all. For a human, he is a force to be reckoned with."

"He may look human, Kira, but he is a bad ass in a very scary and unusual way. We all know that something changed in him on the way here, just none of us understand what, or how those changes will affect him. It's not like we have anyone to ask."

Chapter Two

KIRA

Snacks appearing on hover sleds all around have the boys coming out of the water and what a sight that is.

"We should make a calendar. We would make a fortune," Brit says quietly and all of us crack up. The smirk on DaR's face tells me he knows exactly what I am thinking about right now as he strolls up beside me. I reach over, tracing the water running down his powerful legs.

Alana screeches as SoL stands over her, shaking water off his massive body like a dog. She jumps up, running as quickly as her little legs will carry her across the sand only for him to catch her in two strides. We all laugh as he rubs himself all over her while she acts like she is trying to get away. "Ewe, SoL, … you're all wet … stop it!" Alana is laughing so hard she can hardly say that sentence.

I see DaR look down at me, and at the same time, I hold my hand out. "Don't even think about it, mister." I no more say that than he plops across me, rubbing his large frame all over mine as I am trapped beneath him in this lounger. "Ughh, DaR you brat, get off me your skin is freezing cold!"

"But you're so warm." Wrestling around, somehow, I end up sitting in his lap completely soaked.

"I didn't want to get wet. That's why I stayed up here and you were down there."

"It's my job to take care of you, and you were way too hot."

"I was?"

"Yes, this delectable little body of yours has been distracting me all rising."

"Are you flirting with me?"

"Is it working?"

"I am sitting in your lap, and I don't do that with just anyone."

"I better never catch you in another's lap, or I won't be held responsible for my actions."

"Territorial much?" DaR doesn't answer me, just growls before biting my shoulder gently. I reach over and grab one of the Blood Beets off the tray, handing it to him, before grabbing a purple berry that tastes like strawberry, but looks like a plum for myself. He pulls me back against his chest and I lean back, relaxing in his big arms. The conversations carry on around us, and I allow myself a moment to just enjoy their combined voices.

I must have dozed off at some point because I jerk when I feel DaR pick me up.

"My Kira, I've got you, go back to sleep. I'll wake you in time for the last meal."

I don't remember him laying us down, but he must have decided to nap with me, because his snores wake me up some time later. Rolling over, I pull a light sheet up over us and lay here, watching him. In sleep, his face relaxes, and it's like he is ten years younger. Right at this moment, he doesn't have to defeat or defend the world all around us. After seeing that event on ZoD's planet for myself. I finally understand some of the things he has kept hidden from me all along.

Never in my wildest dreams could I have thought up those damn worm things that had invaded Commander ZoD's home planet. That battle plays back through my mind and I wonder how many times DaR has walked into situations like that one. He has always tried to keep me out of the horrors going on around us, but now that I have seen this with my own eyes. It makes me slightly more cautious, and I have a new understanding as to why DaR is so protective. What is that old saying, *seeing is believing?*

My belly growls and I glance over at the opening that is allowing the cool air in off the water, only to notice that the suns are setting low in the sky so we must have missed dinner. Slipping out of the bed, I tiptoe out of the room, trying not to wake DaR, then whisper, "SAGE, honey, can you bring us a snack? I didn't mean to sleep so long. I must have been more tired than I realized."

"You didn't miss anything, Kira, most remained inside their huts once darkness started to settle. I will have your dinner delivered shortly as I have been holding it in the warmer. Oh, and Luna wants to talk to you about an excursion, but I informed her you were still asleep."

"Is she still awake? If she is, go ahead and connect us. I will take the call out on the deck."

"Let me check."

Luna's face appears as I step outside. "Hey sleepyhead, I was wondering if you were even going to get up today or sleep straight through."

"I hate it when I nap, it makes me all fuzzy, and I feel like I have missed the whole day. It screws everything up, because now I'm wide awake when I should be headed to bed. SAGE said you wanted to ask me something?"

"I think we should take the boys camping. Like backpack camping, you know, rough it for a couple of days."

"Lord Luna, I don't know that I have ever camped like that. What was the word we used, oh yeah, we were glampers. I've always had a camper I could go to when I was sick of the bugs and crap, but I am on board if you think they would enjoy it. There isn't anything like sleeping outside watching the stars."

"Cool, I will finalize it with SAGE and see how long it will take for us to get the tents and things we're going to need here. Just between us, we won't be completely roughing it, but the guys won't know that. I will have SAGE bring us food and all that stuff, but I think we should make this as realistic as possible. Give the guys a little piece of Earth. SAGE said there is a clearing close to a small lake about three miles from here that should suit our needs perfectly."

"Sounds good to me. I will say I am spoiled with my love of creature comforts, but I am willing to rough it for a few days. This is a great idea. I think it will be fun. We'll talk more at breakfast, go on, and enjoy the rest of your evening." Luna throws me a kiss and her face disappears. Darkness has settled fully and just as I turn to go back inside. I see a small figure sitting at the end of the pier, staring up at the sky.

Before walking quietly towards Keida, I check to make sure DaR is still asleep. As I sit down next to her, I instantly notice the tears on her cheeks. Putting my arm around her shoulder, I pull her close to me, rocking her gently as I look up. The sky is so beautiful and clear it almost looks fake. She leans her head against me, sighing heavily.

"Keida, what has you out here all alone?"

"I needed a breath, there are times I feel smothered, and I am so confused. Am I ugly, Mamaw? Oh, never mind, you wouldn't tell me the truth either way."

"What in the world would make you think you're ugly, baby?"

"I think it's obvious. Have you not noticed how Danny has been treating me lately? You would think I have two heads, a split tongue, and a tail or something."

"What are you talking about? That boy adores you."

"No, he doesn't, or if he does, he has a crappy way of showing it. For example, this trip, I had Alana make me this new bathing suit. I didn't want to wear those one-piece things Mom always put on me when I was little. I wanted something a little more grown up. It isn't like I have much to show off, but I didn't want to look five either. The moment I walked out of the room, Danny actually snarled at me. He immediately pulled his shirt off and made me put it on before he would let me out of the door.

"I wondered why you had a shirt on all day."

"That's not the worst of it. See this sundress, I found the design in one of the old magazines ANDI downloaded from Earth. I was in love with the color, cause I thought it would look good with my hair. I wore it to dinner, and everyone, but Danny told me how cute it was. When I asked him what he thought, he said it is ok. He has always been quiet, but every day he is becoming more and more distant. I have often wondered if he stays with me because he feels obligated, or if he really wants to? I would ask him, but I am scared of the answer I might get."

"First of all, young lady, you wear whatever you want and what makes you feel good. Others be damned as far as I am concerned. I am not telling you this because I am your mamaw, but your features are striking, honey. The older you get, the prettier you are becoming, maybe Danny is insecure with that. Let me give you a piece of advice, boys don't think like girls. Our minds are our worst enemies, whereas theirs are very simple and straightforward. Did you ask him why he made you cover up?"

"No, he probably wouldn't have answered me. He is just acting so weird. We have slept in the same bed since we were babies and last night when I turned over to snuggle up with him after a bad dream. I couldn't even reach him because he had tucked the blankets in between us. It made me so mad I almost got up and slept on the couch."

I have to turn away to hide the smile on my face as it hits me as to why he is behaving this way. Danny's attraction to Keida is becoming more than childhood friends, and he doesn't know what to do with those feelings. This is a dilemma because he has no one he can talk to about any of this either. All the guys he is close to worship Keida, so he is lost with these odd emotions on his own. Maybe I should talk to Tyberius and see if he would look at this with an open mind. I sure can't tell DaR or XuL not straight out, anyway. When I look back over, Keida is staring up at the sky. "They are beautiful, aren't they?"

"At one time they were, now I hate them."

"Why would you say that, Punkin?"

"They are going to take him from me and there is absolutely nothing I can do about it."

"Who is going to take who?"

"I would rather not say, if it doesn't make sense to me then it won't to anyone else either."

"Well, maybe not, but it might make you feel better if you did talk about it."

Keida stays quiet for so long that I don't think she is going to tell me, but when she does. I can hear the pain in her voice.

"Mamaw, I've had the same dream over and over for rotations now. I can't pinpoint when, but in my heart. I know one day I will need Danny and he won't be there. The dreams are so real, so vivid. I can smell the dust surrounding us and a weird muskiness from an animal close by. The place is noisy and there are voices everywhere. Out of the corner of my eye, I see Danny reach for something, and just as his hand closes around whatever it is, the stars stretch down from the heavens and absorb him. All I know is he is gone and because I am staring at the empty spot where he was just standing. My own death is just moments away. I never actually see my death, but I can feel it. I used to fight sleep because I didn't want to face this same vision over and over. What I wouldn't do to sleep an entire darkness just once."

"Are your visions always bad, honey?"

"No, sometimes it's just little things. Others, I see … things no one should. I don't always remember them either, and that makes me wonder what is real and what's not. In the past, I would have done anything to make them stop, but my perspective has changed now that I am getting older. I know they are being shown to me for a reason. Usually, it ends up being something that will help one of my loved ones."

Keida gets quiet once again and I ponder on what she has just told me, no wonder she is upset, being a teenager is hard enough without all this. "Zura told me before she left that I am advancing enough in my training to compete in the warrior trials in a couple Orbital rotations, or as you and Mom would say, a few years."

"Is that something you want to do? I thought you had been training all this time simply because you enjoyed it."

"I do enjoy it, being the only girl has its benefits and you're right. In the beginning, I didn't have any real reason to learn, it was simply something to do. However, now … I want to be more than just XuL's daughter and DaR's granddaughter. For some reason, it's like I need to prove how powerful my family is no matter if you're female or male. If this vision actually comes true. I have a feeling this will be a battle I will have to face alone."

"Keida honey, you're right. The girls are highly outnumbered in this family, and as long as you are doing it because you want to, I will be standing on the sidelines cheering you on. I don't know much about these warrior trials you're talking about, but I don't envy you trying to talk your dad into letting you compete, either."

"Hopefully, by that time, Mamaw, Dad will become used to me battling something."

"I wouldn't count on it honey, you will always be his little girl no matter how big or tough you get. If you need proof on how being Daddy's little girl never ends, you should get in touch with Raya. She is Commander ZoD's daughter. Not only is it very apparent she is a warrior, but she is stunning as well. You two would have quite a bit in common."

"Mamaw, … you know, … I am not a big fan of this growing up stuff."

I can't help but laugh. "Baby girl, it's not all it's cracked up to be either. Stay little as long as you can, because once you're big, nothing is ever simple again. You should probably get back. I am sure they are missing you by now."

"Oh, Danny knows where I am. Raven has been watching over us ever since I came out here."

I look around and sure enough, a set of bright blue eyes flash just a short distance away on the main deck. "How did you know she was there?"

"I would love to know the answer to that myself. … I just do, there are voices all around. Some I know immediately. Others … are ones I try to make go away." Before I can ask her more about that she says, "Papaw is waking up, we better go."

Keida is on her feet instantly and sure enough, I no more than get up that DaR walks out of our hut, looking around. A smile graces his face when he sees us moving towards him. "Keida, you look beautiful this darkness, but you need to stop growing. It makes me feel old."

DaR opens his arms, and she walks into them. The love they have for each other is apparent. He kisses the top of her head right before she steps back. Raven appears out of the darkness just as Keida turns. The hound is so large her head is level with Keida's. Keida jumps up, straddling Raven's back, waving as they walk away down the beach towards the hut; they have all been staying in.

"She's been crying, who do I need to kill?"

"Now, Papaw, you can't tear the world apart over a few tears."

"Who says?"

I can't help but smile at the seriousness on his face. He truly would destroy anything that he thought would harm any of us. "Sweetheart, don't you remember being young and the entire world being confusing?"

"No."

"I don't know why that answer does not shock me. Let's just say that for girls this time of life is trial and error. You can't shield her from everything; she has to experience things on her own, that's all part of growing up."

"I don't have to do anything. She is mine to protect and to keep happy at all costs. If something is disrupting that, then it will be removed."

"Lord, help any boys who approach that child, they don't have a chance."

"She is too young to even be thinking about males."

"They grow up quick DaR, and that is something you can't stop. Time marches forward, no matter what. You know she isn't the only one getting older. It just hit me that Danny doesn't really have anyone to confide in, boys' bodies change just as quickly as girls, and he is getting older."

"Tordan has him on a strict workout routine and SCOUT oversees all his other training. He is surrounded by males he can confide in."

"Just because they are working with him doesn't make them his friends, DaR. Danny is alone even though he is surrounded by others. Surely you understand better than most what he is facing, being an only child yourself. Danny only has family members. He can't make friends his own age because you won't send him to public training. Everyone needs someone to confide in, you had Tordan and still do. Who does Danny have?"

"Hum, I will have to give this some thought. The male's powers are simply so powerful that I fear others would take advantage of his youth and inexperience. However, I have noticed he keeps himself apart from the others. I will speak to Father."

"Thank you, that's all I ask. Now feed me, I'm starving and it looks like we've slept through dinner. I have no idea what in the world we are going to do all night. I am wide awake."

"Are you now? I can think of a few things."

"If you weren't so damn cute you would never get away with all that cockiness you know."

"But according to you, I am, so I might as well use it for all its worth. I think you are way overdressed for the activities I have planned for the rest of our evening, let's see if we can remedy that problem."

"Only if you can catch me!" I take off running around the hut and just as I think I have escaped him. He vaults over the roof, grabbing me by the waist before throwing me over his shoulder. Smacking me on the ass, instantly his hand starts wandering up my dress. "DaR, behave yourself, one of the kids might see us!"

"Good, they might learn a few things."

Chapter Three

KIRA

Rolling over, stretching, I can't keep from smiling when I see that the sun has risen quite high in the sky. When DaR feels me moving around he pulls the covers up over his head, and I giggle. "If we don't stop this, we are going to sleep our entire vacation away."

When he doesn't answer me, I tuck my head back under the covers and curl up to his side. His runes pulse lightly across his chest, showing me that he is relaxed. "We are getting too old to carry on like teenagers all night."

"If we were currently that age, we would still be at it, and don't act like you didn't enjoy every moment of it. Several times you were screaming quite loudly."

"Oh, DaR stop it. Do you think the kids heard us?"

"I hope so, paybacks are hell, as you put it."

I smack his chest playfully. "You are terrible."

"No, I am not, but it's a possibility that I am scarred for life. I can't tell you how many times I have come around the corner on Falcor only to have to turn around and head the other way, because one of them is making out right where everyone can see. You simply can't get that crap out of your head … ever."

"Well, the apple doesn't fall far from the tree, my dear. They come by their orneriness honestly. You are absolutely no different."

"That's a matter of opinion. I might start it in the hallway, but I would never finish there. The very thought of anyone seeing you that way would be enough to ruin my mood, or possibly make me rip their eyes out."

"No one ever accused you of sharing well, DaR."

Before he can say anything back, I hear SAGE's courtesy beep. Something she started doing, especially if we were in the bedroom. Pulling the covers back down off my face, I hear DaR sigh. "SAGE we are up, whatcha need?"

"Good rising masters, Luna wanted me to tell you that things have moved up slightly and that we should be leaving in a few hours."

"You were able to get everything here that quickly?"

"Yes. I too was shocked at the availability of the items we needed were here on Targres Four. This planet truly has everything."

"SAGE, I haven't even had time to talk to DaR about this, but I am sure it won't be an issue."

"Mistress Kira, I have also acquired appropriate clothing for you to wear for the trip, and I've packed both of your bags. We will continue to have access to anything that we might need out there, but unlike here, I can't acquire them immediately."

"Honestly, I think that's the point, SAGE. Luna says we are going to rough it."

DaR uncovers his head and sits up, "Kira, what are you two talking about?"

"We're going camping."

"Nahh, I am out. I like it right here. I had enough of that crap when we were in training as younglings."

"Oh, come on, everyone is going."

"Did they know of this, or is it the first they have heard of it as well?"

"They probably just found out. This is something Luna wanted to do with you guys. She thinks it will be fun for you to experience camping the way we did it back home."

Crawling out of the bed, I have to bite my lip to keep from laughing when he growls. "How long do we have to participate before we can leave?"

"I am not certain. Possibly only one night. It really depends on how the adventure goes; I reckon."

"Kira, you know I don't like taking my family into unauthorized locations."

SAGE instantly speaks up. "Master DaR, I have sent Guard bots ahead to secure the area and I will have the shuttle on standby at all times."

He plops back down in the bed and pulls the covers up over his head again. I crawl up over him, pinning his arms down before uncovering just his face. "Don't be a sourpuss. If you expect to have a bad time, you will. Look at it this way, you can show us all your survival skills. If you're good, I promise to act impressed. I may even let you save me from some invisible threat."

In an attempt to appear distressed, I pressed the back of my hand against my forehead and tilted my head back. "Ohhh, save me, my alien commander."

DaR flips me over in the bed, tickling me so hard I can hardly catch my breath. "That was the worst save me act I have ever witnessed. You and the others are lucky I find you so irresistible, or I might simply stay here alone."

"You know, you're not too bad to look at yourself, now get your big ass off me. I am curious to see what SAGE has laid out for me to wear."

"Hump, now clothing is more important than being in the bed with me. I think I am slightly insulted at the moment."

I kiss the end of his nose and crawl out from under him when I hear some of the others talking outside. "Come on, you know it won't be long until they all barge in."

"Who's idea was this family vacation, anyway?" he grumbles out.

"Yours!"

Chapter Four
KIRA

I WALK OUT onto the main walkway in a cute pair of cargo shorts and stylish hiking boots. SAGE definitely took the time to research what we would have worn for such an occasion back home. Most of the girls are dressed the same as I am, except in different colors or slightly more flattering styles. My eyes about pop out of my head when I see Victoria, though.

"Look at those legs, girl. They go clear to your ass. Why in the world would you keep a set like that hidden under all those layers?"

"Stop it, Kira, I am uncomfortable enough as it is. My legs look no different from your own. You simply are not used to seeing me dressed so."

"I can't believe you didn't have SAGE get you an appropriate dress or skirt to wear."

"There is a place for everything, and this was not one of them. Normally, I would avoid these types of adventures, but TY is looking forward to it. He wants to teach the boys how to fish. So, I will suffer the bugs and discomforts for a short while. He asks so little of me."

"Vic, you might even shock yourself and have a good time. This may be the beginning of a whole new wardrobe for you to create." RaZ whistles playfully when he walks by and I can see how uncomfortable it makes Victoria to be exposed so. As I observe her scanning her surroundings, it strikes me that she seems vulnerable, a sight I've never witnessed before. I haven't ever right out asked Vic her story even though there are times I can see the shadows of the past haunting her. It always seems worse if we find ourselves somewhere dark and confined, as simple as in a closet. I no more blink an eye that Tyberius has his arm wrapped around her waist. He must have felt her unease through their bond. The moment he arrives, a small smile graces her lips even though she pulls on the shorts, trying to lengthen them.

"SAGE, my dear, can I have a word with you?"

She hovers in front of me instantly. "Sweetie, is there anything you can do to make Victoria more comfortable?"

"I made sure that the shorts would be the appropriate size, they should be an exact fit."

"That's not what I am talking about, honey. You know she never wears anything that revealing."

"Ohh, yes, her preference is normally a lot more conservative. The shorts have the option of being lengthened to full length. I have the attachments in each of your personal bags. I had them made in case one of you became chilled or if the terrain we are all about to walk through is rough. "

"SAGE, you are wonderful. You think of everything. Would you take the time to show Victoria how to lengthen hers? She may be more comfortable in something longer."

"Absolutely."

SAGE floats over towards Vic and Tyberius and within seconds TY is on his knees helping Victoria slide the extensions over her shoes. The moment her legs are fully covered, you can see her entire body relax.

Strong arms capture me from behind. "You are always doing that. I am a very lucky male."

"Doing what?"

"Looking after another's comfort before ever considering your own."

"I don't have to look after mine. I have you and SAGE to do that for me. It bothers me that Victoria is so self-conscious. She is absolutely stunning. I have no idea what makes her see something in the mirror that none of us do."

"You really don't see it do you?"

"What?"

"She is glamoured. Victoria wears a veil over her appearance. It helps hide the horrors she has lived through. She may appear strong to you and the others, but her true appearance is that of a broken doll. To me, she appears shattered and then placed back together piece by piece."

"I had no idea."

"That's the purpose of being glamoured."

"How is she doing that? I mean, that's kinda creepy."

"I don't know the how's, but Katherine and Father can also change their appearances at will. It was something they obtained on your world; I believe. A true tale of your vampires."

"DaR, I don't know why anything shocks me anymore. At this point, I should just shrug and categorize it as just one more thing."

"Despite the many ways people can conceal their true selves. Kira, you have a unique knack for seeing through most of them. You take on the role of caretaker no matter where you are at,"

"I can't help it, DaR. It pains me to see anyone suffer when I have a way to fix it."

"When I am suffering later, lying on the ground trying to sleep instead of enjoying this nice private room we have here, I will remember that."

"Oh, quit your whining, we won't be on the ground or I don't think so anyway. Maybe I should have asked," but before I can say another word, SAGE pops up in the middle of the walkway.

"If you'll all gather around, I will explain a few things about our upcoming outing."

Chapter Five

KIRA

WE ALL STAND AROUND LISTENING to SAGE tell us where we are going and what's in each backpack. It's almost comical to see the difference in the size of the girl's bags compared to the boys, of course, RaZ is the first to say anything about that.

"Hey, can I cut in a minute? SAGE, we have these things called hover sleds that would pack all this crap to wherever we are going. Why in the world would we personally lug these things anywhere?"

"The goal is to make this as realistic as possible, Master RaZ."

"Well, this pack is not going to fit over my wings."

"It's not supposed to, no one on Earth can fly. So, you are going to walk like everyone else."

"Oh, now that's worm shit. I hate walking, that crap is totally overrated." Before Katherine can say a word, SoL puts a big hand on RaZ's shoulder, looking down at him.

"RaZ, if the trip becomes too hard on you, I will pack you and your little bag. I wouldn't want my big brother to overexert himself."

"Fine, you can just carry me now."

We all laugh as RaZ tries multiple times to jump up into SoL's arms only for him to be thrown into the sky. When SoL first tosses him up, it startles me, but RaZ's response time simply shows this is not the first time these two have played this game.

Tordan grabs his bag off the ground effortlessly, strapping it on, and I watch as he helps Luna get hers settled. "DaR, I will take point; you bring up the rear. Keep all the females between us and have the other males monitor the sides as we proceed forward."

Luna reaches up, touching his chest lovingly. "Tordan, love … this isn't a mission. This is a leisurely walk through the woods with a group of friends."

"I understand the concept, even though I have never experienced it. Still, this area is unexplored and unguarded. We are on an unfamiliar planet with unknowns everywhere. If this trip only included males, things would be different, but you and the other females are our responsibilities. Luna, you know I will not take a chance with your safety, ever."

SAGE pops up in front of him. "Master Tordan, I have downloaded the trail map onto your personal comm unit, as I have all the others at your request."

XuL picks up Brittany's bag, hooking it to the back of his, refusing to let her carry it no matter how many times she tries to take it from him. I have to bite my lip to keep from smiling when she rolls her eyes and turns away, talking to Keida. He smiles because he knows he has won this battle, but instantly turns serious when he sees Hugo.

"Hugo, are there any predators we should be advised of?"

"This isn't my territory, XuL, so I can't provide that information."

I can't help but speak up when I hear XuL ask that. "Guys, we are not going to battle. Everyone needs to chill out." When DaR reaches for my bag, I smack his fingers. "I will hand it over if it becomes too much. I am fully capable of carrying a few things myself, none of us are helpless here."

SAGE pops up in front of me. "Mistress Kira, I will reconnect with you all at the campsite. I have a few things to take care of before I can join the festivities this early darkness."

"That's fine, sweetie."

Tordan's booming voice echoes all around. "This rising is not getting any younger. Load up, males." Tordan doesn't wait for anyone else, he simply starts walking off. All the others fall in line like they have done this half a dozen times. If you were not paying attention, no one would notice the weapons on the guy's hips or the fact that every girl is surrounded. Raven walks calmly at Danny's side as the other three hounds seem to have placed themselves protectively between Victoria and Katherine.

DaR, of course, is only steps behind me. "I really wouldn't want to be a misguided thief or bandit and try to attack this group. The hounds alone would tear them to pieces; you guys wouldn't even have to get involved."

"The hounds are quite impressive to watch. Their movements are almost military-like and they work well together. Their hearing and sense of smell allows them to detect dangers much quicker than we can. It's a comfort having them along."

The terrain changes drastically once we all step off the beach. Not only in temperature, but the scenery. The trees lining the path are much smaller than the ones on Darverius. I have simply quit comparing anything to Earth anymore as nothing I have seen since even comes close. The tree canopy is a kaleidoscope of colors and shapes that shade us from the sun's above. A delicate ground cover of small white flowers lines the path's edge, which seems to be in a zigzag pattern as we approach a hill in front of us.

Hugo and Miya have been chatting quietly in front of me, and I almost run right into him when they suddenly stop. He puts a large red hand out, gathering me close behind him as DaR steps up right to me. Tordan had put a hand up and like a well-trained unit, they immediately stop.

Raven nudges Danny, and I watch as he sits Keida on her back. Tyberius disappears out of sight, but in the blink of an eye he appears behind us. His voice startles me and I jump. "Tordan's comm unit picked up a herd of Bovine ahead and he thinks we should take an alternate route, but it might be harder on the females."

I swear they all should have been in a competition for synchronized dancing. As every one of us girls, are instantly picked up. "DaR, what the hell? And where did your dad go, he was just here?"

"No complaining, my Kira, just sit back and enjoy the ride. And I believe Victoria and Father used some of that famous vampire lore you humans love so well and simply flashed ahead." We will catch up with them shortly, he will comm us if he finds any more dangers. He glances down at his comm unit just as Tordan gives the signal to move on.

The strength these men show without even being slightly winded is amazing no matter how many times I witness it. Tordan, SoL, AvX, XuL, and Hugo, like DaR, are all packing their significant others on one arm effortlessly, while RaZ has Katherine on his shoulders. Raven and the other hounds walk off to the side, keeping all of us between them. My eyes keep coming back to Danny as he walks next to Keida, who is still on Raven's back. You can tell he takes his training seriously as his eyes scan the area around us. It's sad that he might be one of the last human males alive. I don't know if it was a good thing or bad that he was too young to even remember much before being brought here.

It's easy to tell the ones who are used to this type of travel. One of SoL's massive horns has wrapped around Alana from behind and the small horns that line her hair have looped around it, anchoring her in place. Miya's legs are draped around Hugo's waist as he holds her up effortlessly while she jabbers on about the scenery. The fact that she has his complete attention is adorable.

Ivy and Luna look as uncomfortable as I do. I am used to DaR tossing me around playfully all the time, but I don't care much for being packed like a three-year-old. "DaR, my love, is there a reason as to why I can't walk?"

"Are you uncomfortable?"

"Well, no … I understand the terrain is a little tricky and there have been plenty of places so far that you would have had to lift me up onto. Because I would have to climb up something you can simply step onto, but I am not a child."

"My Kira, I know firsthand that you are not a child, but did it ever occur to you that I enjoy having you in my arms? You should know by now that I will take any excuse to do so. As much as I hate to say this, I know you are more than capable of making this entire trip with or without me, but do you really think I am going to let the others show me up? Anyway, it's not much further, so quit your fussing."

"Fine, pack me then."

Chapter Six

KIRA

Leaning back looking up at the sky, I almost miss us entering the large area SAGE found for us, and it's picture perfect with the large lake bordering the clearing. As the guys set us all down, Tordan starts dishing out orders. "XuL, you take the perimeter, RaZ, check to see if there are any threats around us from above."

RaZ lowers the backpack down and Katherin's feet no more touch the ground and he is in the air. His large wings glide effortlessly above us. DaR grabs XuL's and RaZ's packs as we all walk towards the lake shore. "Wow, this place is amazing."

"AvX, will you do us the honors in making sure the lake is safe for us to swim and sleep next to?"

"My pleasure, Father."

DaR and Tordan gravitate towards each other as usual, awaiting the others to confirm that the area is safe. I don't even see AvX go under the water until he comes walking out dripping wet. "The area is clear, Father, there is a large drop-off that everyone will have to watch out for, but other than that it's fine."

I can't help but giggle when I notice that Hugo and SoL are still holding Miya and Alana. The girls are so used to being toted around they don't think to even ask to be put down.

RaZ drops down right in front of me. "Everything is fine from above Daddy dearest." He grabs me around the waist and kisses my forehead only to dart away when DaR reaches out.

"You've got your own girl, get your paws off mine."

XuL walks up next. "Father, it appears that SAGE sent Guard bots out, and they are currently stationed in random areas around us. As far as I can tell, without having the proper surveillance equipment available, the area is secure. So, which one of the females is in charge of this outfit?"

"This was all Luna's idea, but I can tell you that we will need to get our tents set up and a fire ring built for later this evening. I know there are several solar showers that will also need to be filled and hung so that the water will be warm later."

The guys all start walking around the clearing, claiming their spots before emptying the backpacks they had all carried.

Tyberius and Victoria are the first to have everything done, it is apparent that he is a pro at this. His tent and all their gear is perfect, but it goes downhill quickly after that.

I didn't think about each tent being different, but apparently, they all are. DaR pulls ours out of the bag. When I reach over to help him stretch it out, he gives me the look. "What? I was just going to help."

"Kira, I do not require your assistance. I am perfectly capable of setting up this inferior covering on my own."

"Fine, go all caveman on me then. I will just see if someone else would like an extra set of hands." I walk off before he can say another word. Sometimes that man pushes all my buttons.

Ivy is sitting on the ground reading the directions to their tent while AvX is laying out the pieces. Hugo looks as bewildered as DaR did as he holds the small rolled-up tent in his hand. RaZ and Katherin already have most of theirs up, but it's leaning heavily to one side. Tordan and Luna's tent seems to be missing some of its parts, and I can see his mind working on how to fix the issue. XuL and Danny are working together to get their larger family tent up while Keida and Brit hold up the interior until they can get it staked correctly. SoL's boisterous laughter has me and everyone else turning towards them.

Alana is bent over, laughing so hard she is having to hold her sides. SoL got his tent up, but apparently. It's so small, the bottom of his legs and feet are hanging out the doorway. He scoots on his butt back out of the tiny opening with a huge smile on his face. "Is there even any room for me in there?" We all hear Alana ask.

"If I tucked you in the corner. It's a good thing you have me to sleep on, huh?"

"Speaking of having something to sleep on, how the hell are we supposed to inflate these sleeping pads?" RaZ yells out.

Luna holds the one she has been blowing up, showing him the nozzle. "The old-fashioned way; as much hot air as you're always blowing RaZ, this should be a breeze for you."

RaZ grumbles something about *flying back to civilization* before grabbing the large air mattress. "This is a crock of shit, just saying." Katherine must have taken pity on him because she reaches over and takes it from him, within minutes she has their air mattress blown up. He just smirks when she hands it back to him.

I turn back to see how DaR is fairing, only to find him completely done. Our tent is slightly larger than some of the others and through the mesh, I can see the air mattress and the blankets are already in place. Somehow, he has even filled the solar shower, and it's hanging in the direct sun in a tree behind the tent.

"Wow, you're not only handsome, but you're handy, too. How did you get all this done so quickly?"

"I did my research before we headed out. I asked SAGE what type of equipment she packed for us. Then had her download the instructions straight to my comm unit; it ensured that I was more prepared."

"Ohh, using that brain of yours too, you know that is kind of impressive. Where did the chairs come from? No one else seems to have these."

"I sent a few things ahead. The others could have to, but they didn't even try to find a way around the unknowns. They don't call me commander for nothing."

"You are way too full of yourself, mister."

"That's a possibility, but you love every minute of it."

"Yep, pretty much. With all that confidence floating around in your head, don't you think you should help the others out?"

"Nope, come here and sit down, it's the best seat in town. Watching this bunch struggle is a blast, I am not sure who to look at first. It's like watching one of your earth circuses."

"DaR you are terrible," but as I am saying that, I settle down in the folding chair he has set up in front of our tent, and it doesn't take long for the giggles to take over. These are some of the baddest men in existence, but every one of them look completely bewildered. RaZ has attempted to straighten his tent up twice now and it's like the moment he turns his head, it leans back over. All of them are having one issue after another.

Most of them are standing in front of their makeshift shelters just looking around, not knowing what to do next. When Tyberius shows up with two handfuls of fishing rods. They all abandon the task they are working on. "Come on younglings, this is something I have always wanted to do with my family."

Hugo is the first to say anything. "What are those?"

"Fishing poles. SAGE just verified that there are several edible creatures living in the waters of this lake, so we are going fishing. I was going to have you make your own poles, but decided this would be much easier."

Luna and Keida start skipping towards the lake, only stopping long enough to take a pole from TY. None of the boys seem to be as excited as the girls are. When DaR doesn't get out of his chair, I see TY motion for him to come on.

"Ughh, I don't want to go," he grumbles.

"Now, don't be like that, DaR. Fishing on Earth was a way for guys to bond. It was like a rite of passage for a man to teach his son how to fish. Now get your grouchy ass up and go make your dad happy."

"What are you planning on doing?"

"I am coming but only to watch, fishing is a hard no for me. For once, I am going to play the girl card. I have seen enough worms to last me a lifetime."

I grab the blanket DaR had thrown over the back of my chair because he knows how easily I get cold and head down to the lake with all the others. Tyberius is having the time of his life. He has placed all the men a good distance apart from each other and is teaching them one at a time how to use the rod and reel. Poor SoL's hands are so large it looks like he is holding a toothpick, but bless his heart he is still trying his best to cast the thing.

Spreading the blanket on the ground under the shade of a very pretty purple tree, I sit back, ready to enjoy the show. Wishing I had a camera to capture all this. SAGE films everything and I can pick images for her to save, but I still think a camera is more personal.

Luna, Keida, and Ivy all have poles of their own. AvX and Tordan seem to have gotten the hang of it and are casting in and out gradually like TY showed them how to. Then there are Hugo and RaZ, who keep swarping the water with their poles. Several times now I have had to duct down as a lure flies over my head. DaR is holding his pole, but I don't think he is doing much fishing for watching everyone else.

Victoria comes over and settles down with me on the blanket. A small smile on her face as she watches Tyberius walking between each of the guys giving pointers here and there. "He is really enjoying this isn't he?"

"Yes, and it pleases me greatly that we decided to come on this trip. I think we become so wound up in the everyday stuff that we forget to stop and enjoy the life we are building."

"No truer words spoken, girl."

I grab her, barely pushing her down in time, when I see another lure fly over our heads. "I think we are in the hot zone; we might want to move back some." RaZ's cussing gets my attention immediately and within a blink, Katherine is next to him.

"Owww … get it out, get it out."

"Hold still a minute, you are just making it worse. How in the world did you hook your own wing, RaZ?"

"How the hell do I know? My reel is defective, every time I hit the button the line just drops to the ground. Look at AvX, his is all the way out there. I want another one."

"There is nothing wrong with the reel RaZ, it's user error."

Katherine pulls the hook out of his wing and he flares it out, looking so he can see the tiny hole it caused. "Look, I am going to be permanently damaged from this little outing."

"You big pouty ass, you're fine."

"Here let me show you how to do this."

"What makes you such a pro, have you caught anything?"

"I don't even have a pole RaZ, but I don't need one. Watch and learn." Katherine points towards Raven and the hound walks up calmly to the edge of the water. The poles are temporarily forgotten as all eyes turn towards the Hellhound. We all watch as she lowers her head slowly, and I actually jerk as she pounces without warning. When she steps back out of the water, she has a huge, … something that is shaped like a fish, … I think, in her mouth.

Raven throws it up on the bank and then looks up at RaZ. I swear the beast is smiling. "Show off," RaZ snarls at her. "Fine, if she can catch one right here, then I can, too. Stand back and watch a pro get to work."

"You guys better catch something or we are all going to go to bed hungry later," I yell out. DaR frowns and I see him instantly touch his comm unit. I know he just asked SAGE about food, but he doesn't say anything, just winks at me before turning his attention back to the rod in his hand.

Tyberius appears in front of us with a huge smile on his face. "Vic, my love, do you remember what I did with the stringers? I thought I had them in the tackle box I sent on ahead, but I can't find them anywhere. Danny is catching one right after another. We are going to have a feast this evening if he keeps this up. I'm really excited to teach the boys how to filet them."

I snarl my nose at the thought. As I look down the shore, sure enough, I see Danny pull in another one. Keida and him are both laughing as he struggles to bring it in. When Vic and

Tyberius suddenly disappear, I get up to walk around, simply enjoying watching them all together in a more relaxed atmosphere.

RaZ is still throwing his pole like a madman. Poor Alana has had to put her pole down so that she can help put bait on SoL's hook because his fingers are too big to do it himself. Of course, all the guys are riding him about that. AvX is casting like a pro and already has several dead things already lying at his feet. Tordan has his reel in pieces, apparently it wasn't working efficiently enough to suit him. So, in normal Tordan style, it's become a project. Hugo is sitting on the ground cross-legged with Miya on one knee, completely ignoring the bobber he put on his line when he gave up trying to cast, while he gazes at her lovingly. I am not sure where XuL and Brit snuck off to, but they are nowhere in sight.

I smile to myself when I catch DaR watching me, making sure I don't wander too far off. For a split second, I allow myself to see another sunny day like this back home. A day where Rick was teaching Marisa and Cody how to fish. Even after all these years, I can hear Rick's laughter and the sound of their tiny feet running through the house.

Strong arms slide around me, and I blink back the tears not wanting DaR to see them. "Where did you go?"

"Oh, not far, I am simply enjoying the day. I take it you're done fishing?"

"I don't have the patience to stand there all rising. While I can see why some would find this relaxing, it's too slow-paced for my liking."

"Now we are going to starve unless AvX and Danny share theirs with us."

"I believe we will survive until SAGE brings the sustenance later."

"I knew you couldn't resist calling her when I yelled that out earlier."

"If what you had said proved to be true. I was going to have a shuttle come get us. I get cranky when I'm hungry."

"Never … you're nothing but a bubbly ray of sunshine."

DaR kisses the top of my head before whispering, "Only with you. Come on, let's take a walk."

"What about the fish or whatever they are? We can't let them go to waste."

"Father is going to teach everyone how to filet them so they can be fixed later. I had full intentions of ditching that part of this Earth experience, anyway. Come on, let's go see how far we need to walk to escape all their noise."

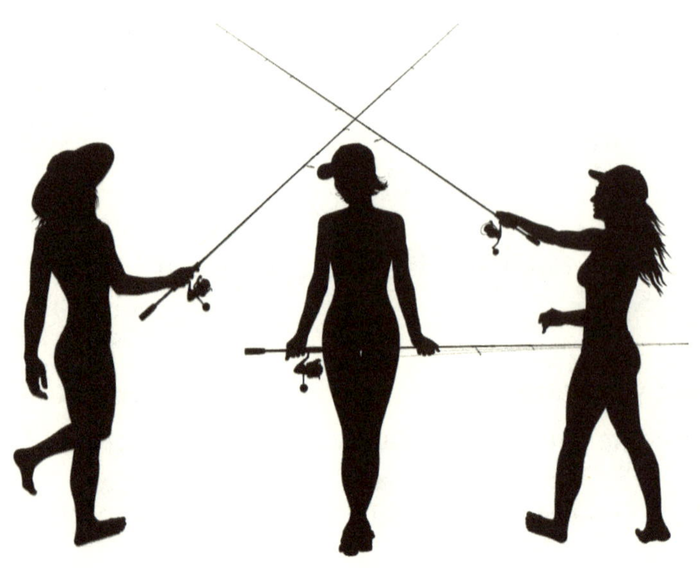

Chapter Seven

KIRA

DaR and I had taken a leisurely walk through the area and we're just returning to the camp when SoL comes around the bend with a frown on his usually smiling face. "What's the matter, honey?"

"I broke my pole." That's when I see the two pieces in his hand. "I was coming back here to try and fix it, but the more I mess with it, the worse it's getting. I was really enjoying this sport, but if it looks like I decide to pursue this further, I will need a much larger pole."

"Stop talking about wanting a larger pole in front of my Kira." DaR says this jokingly, but instantly poor SoL is embarrassed to the point his large cheeks actually flush.

"DaR, stop it. Let me look at your pole, SoL." I give DaR a dirty look, and he turns his head, smiling as I know he was going to comment on that as well. SoL holds it out for me to look at. "Honey, this thing is only good for the garbage can. I don't know if Tyberius brought any more with him or not. DaR, where did you leave your pole?"

"I handed it to Tordan since he had his original one in a million pieces. Darkness is coming and the air temperatures will start to deteriorate. We need to get some type of heat into the area before darkness arrives."

"We are going to build a fire later, but we need to make a secured area to hold it, we are too close to the forest to simply place it anywhere."

"What do you require, Kira? I am available to assist. My Alana was having such a good time I told her to stay with the others."

"We need firewood and a fire ring."

I can see DaR's mind working as he looks around the clearing. "SoL, I will start assembling the fire ring. I believe I saw some small stones near the lake shore."

"Ok then, SoL, how about me and you go gather up some firewood?"

"I would be delighted to help."

"SoL, don't let her out of your sight," DaR growls out and I roll my eyes.

"Come on, SoL, let's go before he wraps me in bubble wrap."

SoL is about as stealthy as a herd of elephants stomping along beside me as we walk further into the woods near the camp. "What type of wood do we require for the fire you want built?"

"Anything dead will be fine, but not rotted, though." He heads off slightly to my right when I bend down to pick up a few sticks. When I turn back, I find him walking towards me with a whole damn tree in his arms.

I have to bite my lip to keep from laughing, but I know how sensitive he is, so I have to watch my words. "Sweetie, that is probably too big. The wood needs to be able to fit inside the fire ring."

He lifts the whole tree up only to break it in half with his knee. "Is this better?"

What do you say to that? He just looks so hopeful. "That will work, but maybe the next few pieces you get can be smaller. It takes quite a bit of small stuff to get a fire large enough to handle a whole tree."

Lord, if I didn't put that boy on a mission. He made two trips for every one of mine, but at least he listened and brought wood of every size from that point on. By the time I stopped him, we could have had a fire for days. I think he cleared the entire underbrush of the nearby forest of any dead debris.

Alana's eyes get big for a second when she sees the pile of wood he has gathered up. "My Alana, will this be efficient, or should I gather more?"

She smiles lovingly at the big softy. "As usual, SoL, you are an overachiever. I think you have worked hard enough today, why don't you come over here and lounge with me until it's time to start the fire. I believe SAGE is going to bring stuff for us to fix s'mores, but is still refusing to bring hot dogs. Once everyone gets back, I think we are going to introduce you all to a few card games."

Chapter Eight
KIRA

Victoria stands up and does her very best to explain how to play the games. You would think with their advanced military minds they would have grasped this easily enough, but nope. If their enemies only knew the game UNO would blow their ever-loving minds, they would have been easily defeated.

I have laughed so hard this last hour that my jaws are hurting, and I can barely hold the cards in my hand. "DaR, my love, lighten up. This is just a game. Hugo is not trying to defeat you in battle."

"The frack he is not; I am not blind to the smirk on his ugly face."

"Huh, ugly my ass. How are you even seeing my smirk, as you call it, over all the cards you're holding in your hand? I am starting to believe that your mind is no longer what it was Commander, and maybe I need to relieve you of your post."

"I am going to relieve you of both of your arms if you lay down that draw four card you're holding in your hand. This game is maddening, Kira. Why would you do this for half a rotation when the odds are firmly against you?"

"DaR, it's just a game, and it's not only you, take a look around at all the other groups. At least one person at every table has a handful of cards the same as you."

"I care not for their circumstances. They're not the ones holding half this deck. I believe someone is cheating."

"There is no way to cheat at UNO. Or, lord, I would hope not anyway."

We all turn when we hear a loud whoop from AvX as he jumps up and down shaking his ass dancing, because after two hours he has finally won at his table. "Losers, take that!" Danny just shakes his head, a small smile on his face as he counts the remaining cards he is holding.

Tyberius yells, "UNO," as soon as he only has one remaining card left in his hand. His leg is bouncing up and down as he looks at XuL, trying to figure out what final color he is going to throw down. XuL appears to be holding half the deck as well. "What color are you holding, Grandfather?"

"Are you trying to trick me, XuL?"

"No, my hands are starting to cramp up and I tire of this color game."

"I need yellow."

XuL never takes his eyes off anyone sitting around him and calmly puts down a … red card. RaZ laughs so hard that he actually falls backwards off the stump he is sitting on. "Good one, big brother. I didn't see that coming, with that color, and since it's my turn. UNO! Love this Earth shit."

Tyberius just grumbles as he starts picking cards up until he gets a red one. "I am cutting you out of my will for that little stunt XuL."

"Hey, what is it that the females keep saying? This is just a game, Grandfather."

I look back only to catch DaR leaning over so that he can see the card in Hugo's hand. I give him a disapproving look when he sees I have caught him and he just shrugs.

Hugo glances back at DaR and I can tell this just got serious. I am about to tell them to put the cards down when SAGE and SCOUT come walking up the trail with two huge Hover sleds floating behind them lined with food.

"Thank the Lord of Light we have been saved from this madness." DaR slams the cards down on the table.

Hugo gets up, stretching his large frame. "I take it that makes me the winner by default?" a huge smile on his face.

I grab DaR by the arm when he turns to say something, "Behave, it was just a game, and I am tired of having to remind you of that."

SCOUT steps around one of the sleds and that's when I notice he is wearing what he would call civilian Earth clothing. "Wooohooo! SCOUT, look at those sexy ass legs of yours." All the girls start whistling at the same time.

Brittany yells, "Damn, SAGE, you better hold on to your man, those legs are lickable."

XuL's runes start to pulse until he looks over at her and she winks at him. Before anyone else can say another thing, SCOUT instantly covers himself in a pair of pants, but a small smile graces his lips.

"Ohh, bummer SCOUT, we were enjoying the view, and did you just smile?" I yell out.

"Ladies, it's not appropriate for you to say certain things towards another male when you are spoken for."

SAGE giggles. "What is it that I have heard the girls say many times? Oh yes, they can look at the menu all they want; they just can't order from it."

"These maddening terms the organics constantly jumble up make entirely no sense to me. No wonder there are so many misunderstandings between them."

"SAGE, my dear, look at all this food, and these trays were an excellent idea."

"I knew the males would need sustenance by now. I do apologize for being slightly later than we originally planned. SCOUT lost Master OrO's signal momentarily, and he refused to accompany me until it came back online."

"Well, he knows how bent out of shape DaR gets when it comes to his sons. So, that was probably a smart move. Were you able to find the ingredients needed to make s'mores later?"

"Yes, I have them in a sealed container, as I was afraid the sugars would attract insects."

"I don't remember who said it, but one of the girls mentioned that you refused to fix hot dogs."

"If they are prepared in accordance with the records ANDI has, not only will I not allow you to eat such things, but I don't believe I could recreate any substance *that* processed. My system simply would not allow me to make anything that unhealthy for the organics I am responsible for."

"I promise we all would have survived. I have devoured several hundred in my lifetime."

"Kira, what is it you tell me to do? If you have nothing nice to say then don't say anything at all. I am using this at this moment."

Chapter Nine
KIRA

Large blankets are placed on the ground for all of us so we can sit on them and eat together. Everyone seems to be talking all at once, but I still hear Ivy ask Brit what her favorite memory of camping was.

"I loved to ride my bike. It was the one place where Mom and Dad would just kinda let me go off on my own. There were always other kids to play with on the playgrounds, and as long as I checked in every now and then, I was free to do whatever I wanted."

"Ugh, humans and the walking thing again. If I remember this correctly, a bike had two wheels that you had to pedal it everywhere."

"RaZ, you don't know what you're missing. These were great moments for a kid."

"Nah, good moments are when your brother can't outrun you because of those puny legs of his and you beat him home and steal his dessert for last meal without Father catching you. Now that's a terrific memory."

XuL reaches up and smacks RaZ on the back of the head and the next thing you know they are both wrestling. I hear DaR let out a painful sigh. "Males, if you make me get up!"

When the boys instantly settle back down. I don't know who is more shocked, me or Brit. Trying to bring us back on subject, I nudge Ivy next to me. "What about you, Ivy? What was your favorite thing about camping."

"Me and Mom only went a few times, but I agree with Brit. Riding my scooter or skateboard around the campground was awesome, but playing on the slides was the best. I always looked forward to the fire later. We were actually camping the first time I saw a shooting star. I was probably about five at the time."

SCOUT turns when Ivy says that. "A shooting star? I don't understand that analogy."

"I don't know the Scientifics of it, SCOUT, but I remember us laying back on an old blanket looking up at the night sky, when suddenly a bright light streaked across the sky. Mom was lying next to me, when we saw it, she told me to make a wish."

"Did this wish come true?" SCOUT asks her innocently.

"I honestly don't remember now, SCOUT. I was just a kid. When I got older, I understood that the random streaks we saw from time to time were comets, or small asteroids burning up in the atmosphere, but as a kid, it was the most magical thing I had ever seen."

"I will have to look into this further, my SAGE might possibly enjoy seeing that as well."

His sincerity and the fact that SCOUT had genuinely transformed into a sentient being in love makes me smile. I mean how damn romantic is that? The evening carries on with more fun conversations and just as dark starts to settle in. I see the boys head towards the immense fire pit DaR assembled in the middle of all our tents. Alana has already made a cute little pyramid in the center of the firepit.

"OK, who wants the honor of lighting the fire on our first family camping trip?"

I see Tordan hand DaR a fire starter and before I can say anything about the fact that we are supposed to be roughing it, the small bundle catches. XuL and Danny start feeding the small flame, making it larger quickly. I don't realize I am chilled until the heat flows around me.

SAGE walks around with an armful of light jackets, handing them out to all the girls. "Thank you, sweetie, you always think of everything."

"You are most welcome, Mistress Kira. Are you now ready for the s'mores ingredients?"

"Yes, SAGE, go ahead and bring them over towards the fire pit. I will have one of the girls explain how to prepare them." I lean over. "Miya, do you and Luna want to tell the boys how to assemble these messy things?"

"Heck, yeah, Kira. I would be happy too. Luna, will you pass out the marshmallows?"

"I'm on it."

"Guys, gather around the fire, you're getting ready for a treat," Alana yells out.

Luna hands out the small sticks and several marshmallows to everyone. Then sits back down next to Tordan.

Alana gets up so everyone can see her. "Ok, take the marshmallow and put it on the stick just like this. Then stick it in the fire. Wait a minute RaZ, I don't mean stick it all the way in, you will get ashes all over it."

RaZ says, "That's what you said."

"You are not cooking it, just warming it up slowly."

None of them are listening to her.

XuL says, "Mine fell off, can I have another one?"

AvX asks, "Why is it bubbling like that? Is it going to blow up?"

SoL comments, "Mine is melting and is sliding down the stick towards me."

Tordan says, "I don't want mine; it smells like charcoal."

Tyberius has a huge smile on his face as he roasts his expertly.

All the guys seem to be talking at once and I can't help but laugh when Alana yells out, "Would all of you stop for a minute and let me show you … Hell's fire." She puts hers on the stick and holds it just above the fire, turning it slowly until it browns lightly. Then picks it off the end with her fingertips, swallowing the entire thing at once.

"See it's not hard, I like mine lightly browned, but you might like yours darker or even burned. Fix several until you figure out what way you like it best before we give you the rest of the pieces to this puzzle."

DaR leans forward and just as he gets his brown Hugo reaches over and grabs it off the end, sticking it into his mouth with a huge smile on his face. "These things are incredible, have you had one yet?"

"No!" DaR growls out.

I pat DaR's leg and laugh as I watch Hugo get up and walk over, gathering up the extra sticks SAGE had brought so that he can fix several at a time. RaZ and XuL are bickering back and forth about the proper way to prepare the marshmallows when Brittany leans over and grabs XuL's off his stick. "Hey, I was going to eat that."

"Snooze you lose."

When RaZ starts laughing XuL turns towards him, and if he had given me that look, I would have peed all over myself. Damn, he can be terrifying when he wants to be.

A gasp from Keida has all heads turning at once towards her and Danny, who at the moment is heating his marshmallow with a bright blue orb in his hand. He turns the stick slowly, just like you should over an open fire, but frowns when it bursts into flames, burning it completely black on the outside. Before anyone can say a word Hugo grabs it, swallowing it in a single bite. "OHHH, these things are amazing no matter how they are prepared."

Keida hands Danny another one and points towards the fire. Reluctantly, I see him lean forward, roasting his like everyone else. The boys messed up so many marshmallows that Victoria and Katherine get up and start fixing the s'mores themselves, handing them out one at a time until everyone has tried one.

"Here's yours, Kira."

"Oh, I don't want one. They were always too sweet for me. You can give mine to DaR. He has been patiently waiting his turn over here."

DaR takes it hesitantly.

"Go on, take a bite you'll love it." Instead of biting it in half. He sticks the entire thing in his mouth. The look on his face after a few seconds is priceless, gagging as he sticks his tongue out at me.

"Ugghhh." He is trying his best to spit it out, but it's refusing to slide off his tongue. "Ugghhh." His poor eyes are watering, feeling sorry for him I reach up and scoop it off with my fingers, now I have this blob of chewed up mush in my hand. He starts spitting on the ground. "Oh, Lord of Light, that's the most disgusting thing I have ever tasted."

Still holding it in my hand I act like I am going to smear it on him and he actually falls out of his chair trying to get away from me. "Lord, if your enemies could only see you now, oh mighty DaR."

"Get that crap away from me. Go wash your hands before it seeps into your skin. Ugghhh, I can't get the taste out of my mouth." Giggling, I walk over to the edge of the woods and flick it off my hand before heading to a wash basin SAGE has on the hover cart. Hugo is all in DaR's face by the time I return.

"DaR, I can't believe you wasted that."

"Hugo, how do you tolerate eating that nasty fracking shit?"

"That explains why you're so sour, you don't eat enough sweets. I have already had SAGE instruct AMI on the production of these delicacies. I can't get enough of them."

Miya walks up and tucks herself under his arm. "Hugo, honey, you might want to slow down eating so many of these at once, you are going to get a tummy ache."

"Will you rub it for me?"

"Yes. You know I will."

"Then let's eat several more, this is a win-win situation for me."

Chapter Ten

KIRA

Darkness has settled firmly; the only light left is what the fire is putting off. I watch as Raven and the other hounds circle around the camp several times before settling down by the fire behind Katherine and Danny. Raven's eyes flash that eerie blue color as she watches all of us. For a moment I wonder what she is thinking about when she looks at all of us. Luna gets up, stepping closer to the fire, rubbing her hands together.

"Hey, who wants to tell a ghost story?"

SCOUT is the first to ask, "What is a ghost story?"

"Oh, it's a camping tradition. When the evening was close to its end and the only sounds around were the crickets and June bugs, storytime would begin. Since this is your all's first time, I'll start, then you guys can go next if you want.

"Four kids and their dog were traveling along in the Mystery Machine when they came to a fork in the road. They didn't notice that the signs had been switched and instead of them heading to their destination, they were now driving down a haunted abandoned road."

Miya starts giggling, "OMG, she is telling them a Scooby-Doo episode; I am dying over here."

"Hey, don't knock it, those stories are classics."

"I am in complete agreement, but you just caught me off guard."

Hugo and the guys all look puzzled, "Are you going to finish your story, Luna?"

"Well, it's not as fun now that Miya ratted me out, but … I bet SCOUT can find it for everyone to watch."

"I am going through the archives I have in my hard drive now." Moments later, SCOUT holds up his hand, projecting the cartoon for all to see. Without all the commercials, it is only about twenty minutes long. I think I enjoyed watching the boys more than the show itself, as they are all mesmerized. SCOUT puts his hand down when the show goes off and instantly they want more.

XuL reaches over, pulling Brittany on his lap. "You mean they made a bunch of those shows?"

"Yeah, Scooby was a popular dog. He had stuffed animals, figurines, and house shoes. The whole world was Scooby crazy."

"When we return home, I would enjoy watching more of these. As enjoyable as this rising has been, are you ready for bed?"

"Yes, we've had a very full day. I am ready to settle down for the night if you are."

XuL stands up, never letting go of Brittany, "We will convene at first light. Danny, Keida, it is time to settle in for darkness."

"Good night to you, too."

Keida gets up off her blanket and runs over to me and DaR, hugging us both before heading towards the tent. "Love you!"

"Love you, baby girl."

Danny awaits her at its entrance, nodding his head towards DaR before heading in with the others. DaR stands up, reaching for my hand. I am sore all over for some reason and it takes me a moment to get my joints to respond. "Are you well, my Kira?"

"Yes, the dampness just stiffens me up, and no, I don't need a healer, so don't ask."

"Mistress Kira and Master DaR, if you are no longer in need of me this darkness, SCOUT and I will retire as well."

"Do you have the perimeter secured, SAGE?"

"Yes, Master DaR, the Guard bots are armed and the hounds are at full alert as you can see them casually patrolling the area."

"We appreciate all the efforts you went through to make sure this outing was a success; you are free for the rest of this darkness."

Within seconds, the blankets are all folded up and on the Hover sleds. Besides Hugo grabbing the last few marshmallows the rest of the food is packed up and whisked away. Everyone is heading towards the little areas they picked out for their tents. That's when I notice that Tordan's is not on the ground. "Where is Tordan and Luna's tent?"

"Tordan said it was of inferior design and he recalibrated the material into a hammock that would hold him and Luna comfortably. If you look up into that tree, you will see it several feet off the ground."

"Leave it to Tordan to completely redesign something so quickly. Lord, I feel sticky all over. Do you think the water is still warm in the solar showers? I meant to take a quick shower earlier, but we were having such a good time."

"The water should be adequate, as it has been warming all rising. However, SAGE didn't leave a privacy screen."

"Oh, we are back to roughing it again. If you'll just hold a towel up in front of me, that'll do."

He growls lightly. "You expect me to stand in front of you holding a large piece of material while watching the water run all over that delectable body of yours and not partake in the temptation?"

"Stop it, you have seen every inch of me for years now. I think you can contain yourself for a few minutes. Anyway, I will have to do the same thing for you, and you are just as yummy."

"You test my limits, female, but we will proceed."

Grabbing the small bag, I packed up here with me. I pull out a small bottle of soap. Then hand DaR the two towels SAGE had rolled up in the bottom. We both head towards the black solar shower and I take my sandals off while DaR adjusts it so that it will flow right above my head.

Switching places, he spreads out the towel, glancing all around. "No one is currently in the area. It should be safe for you to disrobe."

My first instinct is to do this as fast as possible, but his bright yellow eyes devouring my every move changes my mind. Pulling my t-shirt over my head, I slip out of the cargo shorts I have on. Clipping my long hair up out of the way, this leaves me standing only in my matching panties and bra. Turning my back towards him, I slowly lower my bra straps then reach around and unstrap the back closures. Once off, I sling it towards him and he almost drops the towel trying to catch it, but stops himself in time. Instantly his eyes are moving around to make sure no one saw anything.

"Kira, you are playing with fire."

"Nah, unless you plan on packing me off in the woods some-where. I think I am pretty safe from all your advances." I shimmy playfully as I shake my panties off. Flicking my ankle, I send them flying his way and they hit him right in the face before dropping to the ground at his feet. I swear I can feel the heat of his eyes when I reach up and push in the button for the water to come out. I moan as the hot water flows over my cool skin.

"My Kira, have a little mercy on your mate."

"Oops sorry," I grab the bottle lathering up quickly so that there will be water left for DaR to use. Once I'm rinsed off, I turn the water off then motion for DaR. He brings the towel he was holding over, wrapping it securely around me.

"OK, it's your turn," I say, but before I can step away, he picks me up in his arms, kissing me so thoroughly that when he puts me back down, I stumble slightly. Reaching down to get his towel, he is practically naked by the time I get it stretched out in front of him.

I thoroughly enjoy watching the flexing of his muscles as he washes himself under the quickly cooling water. "As much as I love to see you in full glory, love, you might want to put that giggle stick of yours away. You are not the only one who doesn't like to share."

DaR grabs his shaft, stroking it thoroughly and I just roll my eyes as yes paybacks are hell. "Go ahead, get all hot and bothered, it's not like we can do anything about it with everyone so close by."

"You could try to be quiet."

"Has that ever worked out before?"

"No, but we could still try."

"Finish that thing off and I'll be good and stand here." I bite my lip, watching the water run down his chest.

"It's no fun without you." He no more says that, that the water stops running.

"Times up, come here." He walks towards me in full glory. The man's confidence is overwhelming. I wrap the towel around his waist, trying my best to ignore his hardness pressed against my stomach as his arms come around me.

"Behave."

"What's the fun in that?"

Hugo's voice echoing through the clearing has DaR sighing, "That male is a menace."

"Oh, you love him, admit it."

"Never."

"Hey, did you guys enjoy those marshmallows? I sure did, can't wait to get more of those when we get back home. I am not a bit sleepy, are you guys tired? We have got to plan this camping thing again; this has been a blast. Never would I have thought a bunch of squares like you would be this much fun. Are you sure no one has any more of those marsh-mallows?"

Multiple voices scream out, "NO! Now, go to sleep."

"Fine, since you are all old and can't make it any longer. I will simply go to bed myself then."

When Hugo starts humming to himself, I have to grab DaR's arm to keep him from storming over there. "He is having a sugar rush. It will wear off in a minute and he will crash hard."

We stop to look around the camp before getting in our tent. The sight of SoL's massive feet hanging out of the bottom of his tent still gets me tickled. DaR grins when he sees it and just shakes his head before opening up the front of our tent.

It takes quite a bit of wiggling, but we finally get settled. DaR hates it when I go to bed in clothes, but after a little bit, he finally gives up trying to make me sleep naked and lets me put on the small gown SAGE put in my bag.

One thing I forgot about tent camping is the fact that you can hear everything, and I mean everything. Giggles and moans that are cut off by sloppy kisses have me shaking my head. RaZ, of course, is the first to yell anything out; that male has zero filter.

"SoL, you big lug, we can hear you. Keep your horns to yourself."

"Impossible, especially with me being my mate's sleeping platform." Instantly most of the girls are giggling.

"I told you they would hear us," Alana whispers, and the giggles start again.

Things quiet down slightly after that, as the day has worn everyone out. The last thing I remember is a big set of arms wrapping around me from behind, then odd noises wake me up suddenly. DaR turns over and I hear a weary sigh leave his lips.

"I think I am going to go smother the next one that starts snoring. How does anyone sleep with such a racket going on? They are so loud they can be heard on the moons of Sybrus." He no longer says this than our air mattress goes completely flat. I am doing my best not to laugh or even act like I notice, but my hip is lying right on a rock, and the moment I shift to get more comfortable, DaR lifts me up and onto his chest.

"Are we having fun yet?"

"Yes, it has been a fun day full of laughter. I know it's not been ideal, but camping never is. After all, you might not remember the trip, but you will always remember the adventure."

"I could've had just as good of a memory of a nice private bed where I could have ravished you thoroughly."

"I like that idea too. We will do that when we get back to the huts tomorrow. Try to get some sleep, it will make the morning come quicker." Laying my head down on his chest, his gentle breathing lures me back to sleep. I have no idea how long I was out, but it only feels like minutes. Groggy, I can hear the sound of rain coming through the trees towards us.

The rain is light, and the sound is soothing as it blocks the majority of all the other noises around us, that is until I feel a drip on the back of my neck. At first, I think I imagined it until DaR jerks under me. Raising my head up, he shakes his head as a small stream of water seems to be pouring in right above his head. His bright yellow eyes stare up at me while I hold my hand over his face, blocking the stream.

"Isn't this just fracking magical?"

I do my very best to hold back the laughter, but it just spills out. There is no missing the sarcasm in that statement and bless his heart he has been a great sport today. "DaR honey."

"Don't you *DaR honey* me."

"Quit complaining, Father. At least your legs are not sticking out of the tent getting drenched right now."

Tordan is clear on the other side of the camp, and I still hear him say, "I am currently lying in a puddle of water. This design has not performed properly."

Seconds later, I hear RaZ cussing. Rolling off DaR, I unzip the tent slightly to look out, only to see that RaZ's tent is lying on its side. He is sitting outside of its crumbled entrance with one wing stretched out, blocking the light rain off Katherine, who is snuggled up next to him, grinning.

"That's it, get up!" DaR yells out. "I have had it! SAGE, call the shuttle and get us the frack out of here. I refuse to lie here in the rain a moment longer. Girls, this was a fantastic idea, but I am done. At this rate of enjoyment, I am going to need a vacation from my vacation."

"Daddy dearest, I too have stayed long enough. We will see you back at the huts." Katherin barely has time to wave bye, before RaZ launches them into the sky. Tyberius and Victoria come walking out of the edge of the woods where they had set up their tent. Both of them are wearing ponchos, their backpacks neatly folded up on their backs.

"Son, we are heading out, not sure if we will camp again tonight or not, but we are going to explore the area a little more before returning to the huts. We are taking Glory, Ghost, and Thorn with us as they hate being confined in the shuttles. Ladies, you did a marvelous job, I have enjoyed every moment."

"What's all the yelling about, we just laid down." Hugo comes stumbling out of his tent, eyes all red and heavy. "Why do I feel sticky all over?"

Laughter rings out all around at the expense of Hugo who just shrugs his shoulders, grabs Miya, and crawls back in his tent. "You guys go on; we will join you later."

Chapter Eleven

KIRA

It isn't long after DaR's breakdown that I hear the shuttle coming over the ridge. Once it lands, several Cleaning bots are busy folding and straightening the entire area back up so that it will quickly return the way it was before we arrived here.

Just as everyone who is going to head back starts boarding the shuttle. I see Keida poke her finger in the middle of Danny's chest, clearly angry with him once again. Raven is standing at the bottom of the ramp watching and doesn't go on up the ramp until they start walking towards us together. Tordan, unaware of the tension between them, starts talking to Danny as soon as he steps on board. The tears Keida is struggling to hold back are visible to me, but I am at a loss as to what to do. They have a hard journey ahead of them, and it doesn't look like it's going to be an easy one. I am so focused on Keida that I almost don't notice SCOUT suddenly appear.

"Commander DaR, you have an urgent message coming in from Xuias."

"Put it on the holo comm."

Zura's tear-streaked face appears on the screen, but the image is breaking up. Her words are even jumbled, and it takes a second for me to understand what she is saying. "DaR, … you must come right away! They … are going to … execute him … first light."

The holo comm goes black. "Can you get her back online, SCOUT?"

"No Commander, and as of right now. I cannot pinpoint the exact time this was even sent. The message wasn't transmitted through Xuias' open comm system. Zura hacked into a security satellite above their planet to send this directly to me. As distressed as she appeared, I am assuming she was forced to do so, it was the only way she knew for sure you would get the message."

DaR looks back at me. "Sweetheart, do your thing, the girls and I will be fine."

"I will drop you all off safely at the huts before heading there. You are not walking back out of this forest without me. Tordan, XuL?" All he has to say is their names that they immediately jump to what needs done next. Tordan always accompanies DaR on any world issues, but I am going to assume DaR asked XuL because it is his mother's home planet. Xuias is the only planet where DaR had multiple sons. XuL and OrO were both born to Orc mothers.

"Father, I will get the coordinates for the quickest route there and see if I can contact anyone concerning this so that we are not coming in blind to the circumstances."

Tordan simply nods his head before settling down in the pilot's seat. His large hands fly over the panel in front of him as the shuttle lifts off. What took us hours to walk was only minutes this time.

DaR has spent the last few minutes talking to Danny and AvX. I am sure it is concerning the rest of us girls. When the shuttle lands and the doors open. I can tell that Keida wants to ask DaR something as Zura and her have become quite close with her training. XuL must have noticed her hanging back when we were all walking down the ramp.

"Keida, I need you to watch over your mother until I return. I know you have a million questions, but you know as much as I do right now. I promise the moment I know more I will comm you." He pulls her close, hugging her tightly before kissing the top of her head.

Brit stands by, watching a worried look on her face. "You take care of yourself."

"I will return before you realize I am gone."

I don't hear the rest of their conversation because DaR's large hand turns me back towards him. "You stay here and enjoy the time we had left on the rental. I have no idea how long I will be gone, but hopefully, this will be a quick trip. SAGE and SCOUT will keep you informed at all times, and AvX is going to stay close."

Hugging him tightly, I make myself let go of him, each time he leaves it gets harder. "Who do you think Zura was referring to?"

"It must be OrO. SCOUT said that his comm unit isn't responding either. Something must be blocking it, or it's been removed. I have to go, as much as I hate to."

Hesitant, I step back and say, "Be careful and make sure to come back to me. I love you, my big alien man."

"I love you, my Kira."

THE END

Other books from this Author:

Water Skipper Series

Jennifer Julie Miller

The Forsaken series

Forsaken

(Lucas and Emma)

Betrayed

(Tavish and Eve)

Forgotten

(Tyberius and Victoria)

Spin off to DaR.

Darverius, The House of DaR

DaR

(DaR and Kira)

XuL

(XuL and Brittany)

SoL

(SoL and Alana)

RaZ

(RaZ and Katherine)

A House of DaR Celebration (novella)

Tordan

(Tordan and Luna)

Hugo

(Hugo and Miya)

AvX

(AvX and Ivy)

SAGE (novella)

ViN

(ViN and Ember)

SCOUT (novella)

SiN

(SiN and Jade)

Commander ZoD

(ZoD and Tessa)

A house of DaR Vacation (novella)

OrO

I hope ... I have made you laugh, and possibly... even squeezed a few tears out of ya. Writing has been a lifelong dream for me, and our dreams are the only thing we have to build on!!!

So GO for it!!!!

Reading is a passion of mine as well. I believe there are Dragons, Unicorns, and multicolored Kitty Cats, because our imaginations are our own uniqueness.

I am thankful for the support of my family and friends.

To my readers, thank you for encouraging me to continue writing even though my worlds are a little different.

After all, I'm Appalachian, and I talk Appalachian. Therefore, I write Appalachian. All my books have country girls in them, and that's mainly because I only know how to speak country girl correctly.

Then to the Lord above, whose blessing gave a poor little girl from Ironton a chance to dream!

If you enjoyed this story, or any of my other ones, I ask that you take a few minutes of your time, and leave a review on Amazon, or Goodreads. It really helps new and older authors alike.

If you would like to stay in touch, hear about new releases, give some advice, or just drop a line. I love to talk books.

Follow the Author

You can find me on Facebook.

Https://facebook.com/JenniferJulieMiller.

On Twitter.

Https://www.twitter.com/jenniferrick

Or email me at:

Jenniferjuliemiller@gmail.com

Follow me on BookBub. **Https://www.bookbub.com/profile/jennifer-julie-miller**

Follow me on Amazon.

Https://amazon.com/author/jjm5325903

And sign up for my email if you want to learn more about Darverius and DaR's twenty-two plus sons.

https://amazon.us13.list-manage.com/subscribe? u=d6b09705a34917a133b4e5c53&id=64af42f796

DaR

Kira

In the blink of an eye, my whole world has collapsed around me. Headed towards my dream vacation, I was snatched right out of the air. My husband, the love of my life, was destroyed right in front of my eyes. He fought bravely, trying to protect me from a horror neither one of us could have ever imagined. I find myself standing in the spotlight on a stage. Mutilated and tortured, the blood from my body flowing freely down my legs along with my will to live. Piercing yellow eyes emerge from the darkness, but even the shadows can't hide his imposing form. Gentle, but terrifying arms reach out for me and within their embrace, can I find the will to live again?

DaR

I am a bad ass, known throughout the galaxy for my brutality as a ruthless and feared commander. With that being said, somehow, I still got coerced into purchasing a slave. My eyes fall upon a small female whose very essence and eternal light is leaking out of her onto the floor below her. I watch in awe as she accepts her fate, willing her nightmare to be over. I almost turn away from her and the unnecessary cruelly in this room, but the very thought of her dying on that floor surrounded by the very monsters that have done this to her disgust me. I walk up among the beings surrounding her and pull her from the stage, daring, or should I say, hoping, they try to do something about it. The moment I put her in my arms, everything changed. The attachments I have avoided my whole life become unavoidable. Will this damaged slave be able to replace the shadows in my life? One thing for sure is that I will destroy the entire universe to keep her safe. No one touches what's MINE!

XuL

Brittany

All my dreams and wants were stolen from me in the blink of an eye. Awakening, in the middle of a nightmare, I realize I'm being sold like an animal to be studied and dissected in the name of science. Then tragedy strikes, leaving me abandoned and sick. I am only moments from taking my last breath when strong arms pull me from the darkness. I thought it was a blessing that he had found me, the green man who had haunted my dreams. I let myself believe, for just one moment, I might find a small piece of happiness in this unknown world. But what is the old saying? *'Don't count your chickens until they hatch!'*

A blood sucking parasite is eating me alive, literally, and no matter what, I'm not going to survive this horror story. My body is failing me. I beg him to let me go; I just want the pain to stop, but he won't listen. He holds me down and I struggle weakly against his immense strength, choking as blood fills my lungs. When I can't fight any more, Death opens its arms and invites me in.

XuL

My harsh, brutal features have deterred all females, no matter the species. I long for companionship and love. Then I find her, my Kismet, the only one made just for me. The one precious thing I would worship above all others. But the fates are cruel, especially to a male like me.

I am being forced to destroy the fragile bond that has formed between us, as I have to make the hardest decision of my life. One that will make me lose her either way. I hold her small, struggling body against me. Tears flow down my face as she begs me to stop. My heart is crushed as I watch the light leave her beautiful eyes. Upon her final breath, I vow not even Death will keep what's mine.

SoL

Alana

The question is, do I allow this dark moment in time to rob me of the life I could possibly have here? I have never known such horror or fear. If I hadn't experienced it myself, I would have never believed any other living thing could possibly do this to another. The scars may be gone on the outside now, but they will remain forever in my soul. They tell me I can never go back, all that I have ever known is gone. Where does this leave me in the world of monsters? He beckons me, promising me...the fairytale... the impossible dream. Everything I have ever wanted to hear! But I don't know if I'm strong enough to go forward as long as the shadows of our past pull me backwards.

SoL

I knew she was withholding the truth from me. I had no idea who I held in my arms until it was almost too late. The moment her true essence was revealed to me, my body reacted, reaching out for the one thing I had been searching for my whole life… my Inamorata. The very mistress of my heart and now that I have finally found her. I will follow her through the sands of time… no matter how long it takes. I will find my way back to her… because she is MINE!

RaZ

Katherine

How do you go on when all of your wants and dreams have been destroyed? My loved ones were snatched right out of my hands, leaving me alone in a world of unknowns and terror. I'm lost in the in-between with no familiar paths to follow until the sound of a heartbeat and a whisper draws me back to the land of the living.

RaZ

The moment I laid eyes upon her face, I knew there would be no distance I wouldn't travel to make her my own. Unknown forces try to steal her from my very arms and even if I have to fight the very essence of her world, the universe, or the very Gods we pray to. Nothing will stop me from making her MINE!

Forsaken

Lucas and Emma

Katherine's parents

The one question she often asks herself is *why*. Why has she never been enough? Why doesn't anyone truly want her? She was reminded daily that she was nothing but a worthless girl and only another mouth to feed. The last time she saw her family was the night they dumped her in a ditch on the side of the road and left her to die.

A kind woman took her out of that ditch and gave her a home. Her new family was every girl's dream until a single poisoned scratch took it all away. Emma was tossed away again, becoming a prisoner and a slave to her circumstances. The one person the Cook enjoyed beating regularly. The day

Cook sold her body, all of her hopes and dreams were destroyed. But one fateful night, after fighting for her life, she escapes this, Hell.

He finds her on the brink of death, naked, beaten, and barely alive. She thinks he is the Angel of Death, someone who will save her, but he is a real monster. Did she just trade one Hell for another? Will the memories he steals from her dreams soften his heart enough to make him care for something more than himself? Or will he turn her away, just to *Forsake* her, like all the rest?

Betrayed

Tavish and Eve

It seems the ones we love the most are the first to Betray us!
One such Betrayal cost me everything: my home, my dreams,
and almost my life. The second I started running, I knew I
would never be who I was or may have wanted to be. All of
my choices were taken away with two last breaths, hers and
then my own.

The dreams of my youth were destroyed because of the self-
ishness of others. I fear my life will become nothing but a cold
existence of shadows and detachment.

The poison consuming my very soul is nothing but an excuse
for me to lash out at the unfairness of it all. It's exactly the
justification I need to deliver the pain others have inflicted on

me my entire life. Will the emotions of my untried youth destroy my future as I'm forced into a world I truly don't understand?

My own mind has become my worst enemy, and my fragile heart can't withstand another break. I know he's a deceiver, a devil in disguise, sent to collect my grieving soul. He is the real monster my mother warned me about under the bed. If I let him, he will destroy me in the end with his mischievous smile and lying angel eyes.

To be loved is the only dream I have left, but we all know Betrayal is the one thing you can always count on to crush you.

Forgotten

Tyberius and Victoria

(DaR's father)

I have known this evil was coming for me my whole life, but that doesn't mean I have looked forward to it! I have run from every sign of the darkness, even to the point of being invisible to the ones around me. I've spent my whole life lurking in the shadows of my family. Keeping myself separate from the ones I love, living my dreams, and wants through their eyes.

I had become so wrapped up in their worlds trying to ensure their happiness that the day he appeared in front of me. I never once questioned what I was supposed to do. The one thing my family could always count on is that I'm loyal to fault. Even though I made sure never to get too attached because I was terrified the darkness would take them also, it will do anything it can to defeat me. My goal is to survive and to finally see the light.

I have prayed to every God, for this to pass me by, only to know they can't answer. This is my destiny. I will suffer agony unlike anything my mind can imagine, but to be worthy of the light. I need to find a way to face this darkness.

I will never show him an ounce of weakness, but I scream silently for help. I refuse to let him win because he wants me here for eternity. A soul withered in ice, and loneliness, Forgotten in this room of horrors.

All the stars line up for us one time or another. I just have to wait my turn.

Tordan

Luna

They stole my dreams, my hopes, my very identity, and I had no idea. Years went by and I did everything I was told, I was always the perfect specimen, and the perfect lab rat. I was dissected, even maimed all in the name of science. Then one day a strange smoky voice entered my head, and I knew things were not as they seemed. He promises me that he will never leave me, but my new memories tell me differently.

Tordan

What is it about that one person that attracts you like no other? My mind can't figure out that riddle, but the moment I laid eyes upon her I knew my life would never be the same. When I finally held her in my arms, I swore I would never be without her again. If they think they will get me to comply by using her to control me, they're right. What they don't know is…I will tear this compound, and all that's in it apart, to protect what's MINE.

Hugo

Miya

I awaken to the touch of cold metal hands and talking holograms. Paralyzed and dependent on the Others. They tell me a story… at first; I refuse to believe. A story of no return and extreme loss, but one of the voices is different. He projects anger and distrust…but his hands… even though cold and hard, are always gentle. I have come to crave the sound of his growls because I know within moments he will hold me in his arms. When my sight returns. I was not prepared to see what he really was, but when he collapsed in front of me, his body failing. Why do I suddenly feel like this is my biggest loss yet?

Hugo

I have done everything in my power to prepare a safe world for her once I'm gone. I fought my attraction, knowing I was unworthy of her trust, but I crave her like no other. Unfortunately, my mind is no longer my own, and the only way to destroy the monster who has invaded my head is death. All that matters in my end... is that she survives... because I would rather die than share what I know is MINE.

The Playboy and the Waitress

Jenna

I was always told never to forget that I was worth something, too! We all know that every little girl dreams of her knight in shining armor. A man who will ride up and save her from the evil things trying to destroy her. Then, of course, we all know they live happily ever after. My knight was untouchable... A Playboy, a man who stole my heart right out of my chest and with very little effort on his part. Unfortunately, he was also a man whose world I would never fit in. You can take the girl out of the country. You can dress her in nice clothes, have her smile beautifully as you parade her on your arm, but you never really take the country out of the girl. I reach out for the brightest of stars... only for him to leave my heart in pieces, crumbling at my feet.

Dage

I watched her for weeks. Every smile she bestowed on me captured me in a way no others had. Circumstances throw us together over and over and no matter how many times I hold her in my arms, it's never enough. I didn't know what I was missing until she walked away. I know, I can't have them and her… so who will lose?

AvX

Ivy

Why are the last words ever spoken to our loved ones is in anger? I knew the moment I left it was a mistake, but my stubborn pride urged me forward. I've awakened to unimaginable horrors, pain unlike anything the human mind could conceive, until him. Now, I'm too scared to trust my own feelings, as they have only led me astray. I push his kindness away, striking out in a rage of harsh words and unwarranted anger. As this new future is revealed to me, I crumble away inside,… slowly and insidiously. How much more do I have to lose before I realize my sole chance of happiness is standing in front of me?

AvX

She is like a wild animal, cornered and frightened, unwilling to accept any sort of kindness. A fiery soul trapped inside a mind littered with insecurities and heartache. I ache for a kind word or a gentle touch as my body reacts to her slightest touches. How do I convince her to put aside the pain she has endured and take a chance on the unknown,... on me? The fates put her in my path for a reason, and I will find a way to tame the fire that consumes her.

Sage

SAGE

I was forced to make a decision, her life for mine. It really was a simple question to answer because at the end of the day, I'm nothing more than a wanna be girl, with the dream of being more.

SCOUT

She doesn't see her own worth, but I will streak through the cosmos to protect her.

ViN

Ember

I was separated from my parents and a world where the most important thing I had to worry about was my next outfit. Everything I have ever been or will be… torn away abruptly as I'm thrown into what feels like never-ending chaos and confusion. Thrust upon an Alien male who I can't understand and dangers I don't comprehend. How do I cope with the reality of being alone on an alien planet where I'm not wanted?

ViN

I live for the next mission, with absolutely no need for a female of any kind. Until a whiny, ungrateful, high-maintenance one falls literally into my arms. Why does the feel of her small body and the urge to make her smile again confuse me? Fighting the attraction and refusing to be like the others. I walk away from the temptation, so why do her tears haunt me so?

Scout

SAGE

The ultimate betrayal on his face when he sees that plug in my hand shatters my cybernetic heart. Helpless, my world turns to chaos, and I spiral downward, crushed by my very own actions.

SCOUT

Trying to be the hero, I lost it all without even knowing it. The world went on without me. However, our love proved to be stronger, and apparently, the gods were not done with me yet. With me gone, an unlikely partnership forms risking it all to bring me back, but will it be me, or something else that emerges.

SiN

Jade

I find him injured, a monster hiding in the shadows of an unknown, terrifying world. When I run from him, I end up thrust into the middle of an unbelievable war full of creatures I can't fathom exist. My sole worth in the eyes of these warmongering beings is as a sacrifice on the altar of destruction. My mind and body crave what only he can give, but the darkness harbored within his soul frightens me. Resigned to my fate, I prepare myself to draw my last breath; I dream he will come, but we all know dreams never come true.

SiN

I am the thing of nightmares hiding under the bed. The monster lurking in the shadows, haunting the worlds I travel.

This is who I am, or was until I opened my eyes and saw her. My Angel. Everything I've ever known, everything I've been taught my entire life, has been a filthy lie. In my usual fashion, I refuse to believe the facts and react without remorse for those around me. Now, because of my crimes and past transgressions, I might be too late to save my guiding light. She's the only thing that can deliver me from the darkness I've become enshrouded with.

ZoD

ZoD

Failing my people is not an option and I'll do whatever is needed to make sure that doesn't happen, that is until she runs into my arms. Now the universe be damned because I will sacrifice them all to keep her safe. My very soul reaches for her, but no matter how hard I fight to get to her. My *Amouri* is just out of reach. Will she ever come to terms with the things that have been forced upon her? Will she finally see the male that is standing right in front of her? Or will my fears push her away?

Tessa

I closed my eyes in one world only to open them in another. Terrified and disoriented, I flee, only to find myself trapped in an enormous embrace of the universe's largest arms. Now I am in a world I don't understand, surrounded by others who are leery of their master's new pet. He says all the right words, but am I brave enough to let go of the past and trust what he says is true? Can I turn my back on all that I knew just because I am here now? Or will the creatures hunting them all take my choices away?